INTER MIAMI

Inter Miami Chronicles From Vision to Victory

Louis L. Legge

Inter Miami

All rights reserved. No part of this publication may be reproduced, distributed, or transmitted in any form or by any means, including photocopying, recording, or other electronic or mechanical methods, without prior written permission of the publisher, except in the case of brief quotations embodied in critical reviews and certain other noncommercial uses permitted by copyright law.

Copyright © Louis L. Legge, 2024.

TABLE OF CONTENTS

INTRODUCTION

Inter Miami Chronicles From Vision to Victory
In vibrant downtown Miami, where the rhythm of the streets reflects the passion of its residents, a soccer revolution was born. This is the story of Inter Miami CF, a story that transcends the boundaries of sports and encapsulates the spirit of a team that dares to dream, envision greatness, and pursue victory against all odds. "Inter Miami Chronicles: From Vision to Victory" invites you to immerse yourself in the riveting story of a club that emerged from the sandy shores of South Florida to leave a lasting mark on the Major League Soccer landscape. Beyond the dazzling lights of the Miami skyline and the allure of its world-famous beaches, Inter Miami's journey unfolds as a testament to determination, ambition, and the relentless pursuit of excellence. This column takes you on a fascinating

journey, exploring how Inter Miami came to be, the strategic moves that shaped its destiny and the key moments that defined its path from the dream of those with foresight to the sweet taste of victory on the football field. From the iconic pink jerseys to the passionate fans, each element contributes to the unique tapestry that is Inter Miami FC. Join us as we explore behind-the-scenes stories, share triumphs, and reflect on the challenges faced by this pioneering football club. This book not only recounts the wins and losses but is also a tribute to the indomitable spirit that fueled Inter Miami's rise. As we turn the pages of the Inter Miami Chronicle, let us bask in the bright colors of victory, the nuances of perseverance, and the unwavering faith that turned a vision into a legacy. The journey was waiting for him and the victory was recorded in the annals of Inter Miami.

CHAPTER 1: WHO ARE INTER MIAMI CF

Is a professional soccer club based in Miami, Florida that competes in Major League Soccer (MLS), the top soccer league in the United States. The club was officially announced as an MLS expansion team in January 2018 and began competing in the league in the 2020 season. Inter Miami is one of the newest additions to MLS and is owned by a group of investors, including notable figures such as David Beckham, Marcelo Claure, Jorge and Jose Mas, and Masayoshi Son.

David Beckham

Famous former English footballer and international football icon, David Beckham was a central figure in the founding of Inter Miami CF. He was the driving force behind the vision of bringing professional soccer back to Miami. Beckham's involvement in the project includes his role as owner, promoter, and ambassador of the club.

Inter Miami

Although Beckham is a prominent figure, it is important to note that the ownership structure and establishment of sports clubs can involve many individuals, investors, and organizations.

Jorge Mas

Co-owner and manager of Inter Miami CF. Jorge Mas is a successful businessman and entrepreneur with a strong presence in Miami. He is the Chairman of MasTec, a multinational infrastructure engineering and construction company. Jorge Mas played a key role in the effort to bring Major League Soccer (MLS) to Miami. His involvement, along with other notable figures including David Beckham, was instrumental in the creation of Inter Miami CF. In addition to his business acumen, Jorge Mas also brings strategic vision and local knowledge to the club. His understanding of the Miami market and commitment to community engagement have helped shape the identity and direction of Inter Miami CF. Jorge Mas is known for participating in community initiatives, his contributions extend beyond football, reflecting his commitment to making a positive impact on the local community.

Jose Mas

Famous businessman and one of the key figures associated with Inter Miami CF, a Major League Soccer (MLS) team based in Miami, Florida. José Mas is one of the co-owners of Inter Miami CF. His involvement in the ownership group, along with other notable figures such as David Beckham, Jorge Mas, and Marcelo Claure, was instrumental in the creation and development of the football club. He is the CEO and Chairman of MasTec, a multinational infrastructure engineering and construction company. MasTec operates in a variety of sectors including energy, telecommunications, and utilities. His experience in business development and infrastructure brings valuable expertise to the ownership group. Together with the ownership group, he expressed his commitment to community involvement and initiatives throughout Inter Miami CF. The club has actively participated in programs and projects to create a positive impact on the local community. José Mas is the older brother of Jorge Mas, another key figure in the group that owns Inter Miami CF. The involvement of the Mas family in the ownership structure underlines a shared commitment to the success and development of the football club. The ownership group, including Jose Mas, has created a vision for Inter Miami CF that goes beyond success on the field. Their aspirations include creating strong and lasting connections with Miami's diverse community and contributing to the growth of soccer in the region. In addition to Inter Miami CF, he is also involved in various community projects and initiatives in the Miami area. This reflects a wider commitment to making a positive contribution to the development and well-being of local communities. As co-owner, he contributes to strategic decision-making and leadership of Inter Miami CF. His involvement extends to key aspects of the club's operations, including stadium development, commercial partnerships, and community outreach.

Marcelo Claure

He is an investor and co-owner. His role is part of the ownership group, which includes other notable figures such as David Beckham, Jorge Mas, and others. He has been involved in various business projects and held management positions. He is the Chief Executive Officer (CEO) of SoftBank Group International, a position that involves overseeing SoftBank's international operations. SoftBank Group is a multinational corporation headquartered in Japan. She has various business interests including telecommunications, internet services, robotics, and technology investments. Marcelo Claure's role at SoftBank has allowed him to gain significant experience in the global business landscape. Before joining SoftBank, Marcelo Claure served as CEO of Sprint Corporation, a large telecommunications company. He played a key role in leading Sprint through a period of industry transformation. He has a history in business, having founded and operated many different businesses. His experience includes telecommunications, technology, and other sectors. He has been involved in philanthropy and community engagement initiatives. His contributions extend beyond business to projects and programs aimed at positively impacting the community. In addition to commercial activities, Marcelo Claure's involvement with Inter Miami CF reflects an interest in sports and football. His role as an investor underlines his commitment to the football club's growth and success.

Masayoshi Son

He founded SoftBank in 1981 and has served as Chairman and CEO since then. Under his leadership, SoftBank has become one of the largest and most diverse technology and investment companies in the world. SoftBank Group has various business interests including telecommunications, technology, e-commerce, robotics, and investments in various companies and startups worldwide. SoftBank's Vision Fund, headed by Masayoshi Son, is known for its significant investments in technology companies. He founded the SoftBank Vision Fund, one of the world's largest technology investment funds. The Vision Fund has made significant investments in technology companies, including those involved in artificial intelligence, telecommunications, and e-commerce. SoftBank Group, under the leadership of Masayoshi Son, has invested in various industries, including sports and entertainment. This includes investments in sports teams and companies, in line with Masayoshi Son's broader business interests. Masayoshi Son has a long history as a businessman and has been involved in various business activities since the beginning of his career. His ability to identify emerging technologies and trends has been key to SoftBank's success. In addition to business, he also expressed interest in using technology to solve social challenges. SoftBank's initiatives include investing in renewable energy and technology to improve people's lives. He is known as one of the investors of Inter Miami CF, a Major League Soccer (MLS) team based in Miami. His participation will add financial support and strategic knowledge to the ownership group. Masayoshi Son has been involved in philanthropic efforts, contributing to various causes globally. SoftBank Group is committed to initiatives focused on social impact and sustainability.

1.1: Early years of soccer in Miami

Soccer in Miami was checked by the city's section into the North American Soccer Association (NASL) in the 1970s and 1980s. Here's a brief outline of the early long time of soccer in Miami:

NASL Development:

Within the mid-1970s, Miami saw the development of proficient soccer with the foundation of the Miami Toros within the North American Soccer Association (NASL). The NASL was the top-tier soccer association in the United States during that period.

Miami Toros (1972-1976):

The Miami Toros, established in 1972, became the primary proficient soccer group in Miami. They played their domestic matches at the Tamiami Stadium. The group had eminent players and picked up neighborhood bolster amid its presence within the NASL.

Post Lauderdale Strikers:

Whereas not based in Miami, the Fortification Lauderdale Strikers, another NASL group, played a noteworthy part in the soccer scene of South Florida. The contention between the Miami Toros and the Post-Lauderdale Strikers included fervor for the neighborhood soccer scene.

Tamiami Stadium:

Tamiami Stadium, found in West Miami, served as the domestic scene for the Miami Toros amid their NASL for a long time. The stadium played a central part in facilitating proficient soccer matches and contributing to the development of the don within the locale.

Bequest of NASL Period:

The NASL's time in Miami laid the groundwork for professional soccer within the city. Whereas the Miami Toros had a moderately brief existence (disbanding in 1976), the effect of their nearness lingered, contributing to the establishment of soccer culture within the region.

Post-NASAL Period:

After the disintegration of the NASL in the 1980s, proficient soccer in Miami experienced a period of torpidity. The nonattendance of a proficient group during this time did not diminish the energy for soccer among the neighborhood community.

Worldwide Soccer Occasions:

Indeed amid periods without a nearby proficient group, Miami proceeded to host worldwide soccer occasions including noticeable clubs and national groups. These occasions fueled the intrigue and excitement for soccer within the locale.

Whereas the NASL period of the Miami Toros was generally short-lived, it laid the basis for the soccer bequest in Miami. The consequent long time saw the rise and drop of distinctive soccer activities, driving the possible foundation of Inter Miami CF in Major Association Soccer (MLS) in 2020, stamping a modern chapter within the city's soccer history.

1.2: Miami Combination (1997-2001)

The Miami Combination was a Major Alliance Soccer (MLS) group that operated from 1997 to 2001. Here are key focuses almost the Miami Combination amid its presence:

Formation and Inaugural Season (1998):
The Miami Fusion was one of two expansion teams included in MLS for the 1998 season, together with the Chicago Fire. The group played its domestic matches at Lockhart Stadium in Post Lauderdale.

Group Colors and Symbols:
The Miami Fusion's group colors were orange, blue, and yellow. The symbol included a stylized delineation of a soccer ball with palm trees, reflecting the South Florida setting.

Victory on the Field:
The Fusion accomplished eminent victory on the field amid its brief presence. Within the 2001 season, under

the coaching of Beam Hudson, the group wrapped up to begin within the Eastern Conference and come to the MLS Glass Playoffs.

Outstanding Players:
The Miami Combination list included eminent players such as Preki, Carlos Valderrama, and Diego Serna. These players contributed to the team's victory and cleared out a lasting effect on the establishment.

Domestic Venue - Lockhart Stadium:
Lockhart Stadium in Fortification Lauderdale served as the domestic scene for the Miami Combination. The stadium had a capacity of around 20,000 onlookers and was shared with the
Post-Lauderdale Strikers

.

MLS Supporters' Shield (2001):
The Miami Combination accomplished a significant milestone within the 2001 season by winning the MLS Supporters' Shield, granted to the group with the finest regular-season record.

Suspension and Withdrawal (2002):
Despite an on-field victory, the Miami Combination confronted money-related challenges and battled with participation figures. In a questionable move, MLS chose to contract the team along with the Tampa Inlet Uprising after the 2001 season. This choice pointed to streamlining the league and addressing financial concerns.

Bequest and Affect:
The Miami Fusion's bequest incorporates its contribution to the development of soccer in South Florida and its victory on the field. The team's withdrawal stamped a challenging period for soccer devotees within the locale.

Post-Fusion Soccer in Miami:
After the withdrawal of the Miami Combination, the locale experienced rest in proficient soccer until the foundation of Inter Miami CF in Major Association Soccer in 2020. The Miami Fusion's time in MLS cleared a permanent check on the history of soccer in

Miami, and its legacy is remembered by fans who saw the team's accomplishments amid its long time of operation.

CHAPTER 2: THE BIRTH OF A SOCCER VISION IN MIAMI

1. Colors: Inter Miami's colors are dark, pink, and white. The club's peak highlights two herons, symbolizing opportunity, style, and quality. Inter Miami CF's essential colors are dark, pink, and white. The combination of these colors is particular and stands out within the world of soccer. The choice of pink, in particular, is special in soccer and has become a signature component of the club's personality.

- Dark:

Dark is one of Inter Miami CF's essential colors, speaking to quality, modernity, and a sense of polished skill. It is frequently included within the club's packs, stock, and branding materials.

- Pink:

Pink could be a standout and flighty color choice for a soccer club, making Inter Miami CF effectively recognizable. The utilization of pink symbolizes dynamic quality, vitality, and the exuberant soul of

Miami. The pink shirts have ended up notorious and are broadly related to the club.

- White:

White is another essential color utilized by Inter Miami CF, giving differentiation and adjusting to dark and pink. White is regularly seen within the team's shirts, and it complements the other colors, contributing to a clean and cutting-edge taste.

These colors do not as it were to frame the visual personality of Inter Miami CF but moreover reflect the energetic and assorted social air of Miami. The consolidation of pink, in particular, sets the club apart from conventional color plans in soccer, including a sense of pizazz and uniqueness to Inter Miami CF's branding and general picture. If it's not too much trouble, note that subtle elements about the club's colors may be subject to alteration, and it's prescribed to check official club sources for the foremost up-to-date data.

2. Peak: Plays a significant part in establishing the visual personality and acknowledgment of Inter Miami CF. It

typifies the essence of the club, combining components of nature, imagery, and a cutting-edge plan stylishly.

- Herons:

The central feature of the peak could be a combination of herons, and exquisite fowls with outstretched wings. The herons are situated back-to-back, making a symmetrical and energetic composition. Herons are known for their beauty and flexibility, symbolizing flexibility and quality.

- Shield Shape:

The crest is molded like a shield, a common plan in soccer club peaks. The shield fortifies a sense of character, solidarity, and convention. It gives a visual system for the club's typical components.

- Color Palette:

The peak joinsInter Miami CF's essential colors—black, pink, and white. These colors are utilized deliberately to improve the visual request and in general taste of the peak.

- Content:

The club's title, "Inter Miami CF," is ordinarily included within the peak. The typography utilized for the title contributes to the, by and large, plan, guaranteeing neatness and cohesion with the other components.

- Symbolism:

The herons within the peak are more than enriching; they carry symbolic noteworthiness. Herons speak to flexibility, flexibility, and the energetic soul of Miami. The choice of this fowl reflects the club's association with the nearby environment and its goals.

- Club Witticism or Trademark:

Some club peaks incorporate a witticism or trademark that typifies the team's values or mission. In case Inter Miami CF contains a particular proverb, it may be joined into the peak

- Sun:

In a few emphases of the peak, there's a representation of the sun behind the herons. The sun includes a touch of warmth and complements the topic of the energetic Miami soul.

3. Stadiums: At first, Inter Miami played its domestic matches at the Inter Miami CF Stadium (also known as DRV PNK Stadium) in Post Lauderdale. The team's

long-term home is planned to be Miami Flexibility Stop, a proposed complex that incorporates a soccer stadium, preparing facilities, and more. Inter Miami CF initially played its inaugural season domestic matches at Inter Miami CF Stadium (once in the past known as Lockhart Stadium) in Fortification Lauderdale whereas DRV PNK Stadium was under construction. However, DRV PNK Stadium became the club's lasting domestic stadium upon its completion. Data approximately DRV PNK Stadium:

- DRV PNK Stadium:

Area:

1350 NW 55th St, Fort Lauderdale, FL 33309, Joined together States

- Capacity:

The stadium features a capacity of around 18,000 seats.

- Highlights:

DRV PNK Stadium may be a soccer-specific stadium outlined to form an insinuating and vibrant climate for soccer matches. It features cutting-edge offices, conveniences, and fan-friendly housing.

Inter Miami

4. Inaugural Season: The group debuted in MLS within the 2020 season, stamping its beginning with official competitive matches. The inaugural season was noteworthy for the Inter Miami CF, an extension group in Major Association Soccer (MLS), played its inaugural season in 2020. The 2020 MLS season stamped the club's passage into the association, and it was a memorable year for Inter Miami CF. In any case, the group confronted a few challenges in its, to begin with the season, the establishment of Inter Miami CF checked a significant minute within the development of soccer in Miami. The club laid the establishment for future seasons, contributing to the dynamic quality of the MLS and the soccer scene in South Florida. The club laid the establishment for consequent seasons, building on its identity, fanbase, and yearnings within the competitive landscape of Major Association Soccer.

- Arrangement and Section into MLS:

Inter Miami CF authoritatively entered Major League Soccer (MLS) as an expansion group for the 2020 season, joining the league's nearby individual development group Nashville SC.

Inter Miami

Possession and Authority:

The possession bunch, driven by David Beckham, Jorge Mas, and other unmistakable figures, played an essential part in forming the vision and heading of the club.

- Head Coach - Diego Alonso:

Diego Alonso was named as the head coach for Inter Miami CF's inaugural season. Alonso brought involvement and a fruitful track record to direct the group.

- Domestic Matches at Inter Miami CF Stadium (Lockhart Stadium):

Due to the continuous development of DRV PNK Stadium, Inter Miami CF played its domestic matches at Inter Miami CF Stadium, which was arranged at the historic Lockhart Stadium site in Post Lauderdale.

- Make a big appearance Coordinate and To begin with Victory:

Inter Miami CF played its first-ever MLS match on Walk 1, 2020, against Los Angeles FC (LAFC). The memorable coordinate finished in a 1-0 triumph for LAFC. Inter Miami CF secured its first victory afterward within the season.

- DRV PNK Stadium Introduction:

DRV PNK Stadium (once in the past known as Inter Miami CF Stadium) was introduced afterward within the season, serving as the club's permanent home scene.

- Performance and Playoff Thrust:

Inter Miami CF confronted challenges amid its inaugural season but appeared to advance as the season progressed. The group made a late push for a playoff spot within the Eastern Conference.

- Striking Signings:

All through the season, Inter Miami CF made eminent player signings, counting assigned players like Rodolfo Pizarro and Blaise Matuidi, including to the team's competitiveness.

- Adjusting to MLS:

As is common for extension groups, Inter Miami CF went through a learning bend, adjusting to the competitive nature of MLS. The group worked to set up its playing style and construct cohesion.

- Effect of the COVID-19 Pandemic:

The 2020 season was affected by the COVID-19 pandemic, driving alterations within the plan and the introduction of safety conventions to ensure players and staff.

5. Community Engagement: The club strives to associate with the differing population of Miami and contribute emphatically to the neighborhood community through different programs and outreach endeavors. Community engagement is a noteworthy aspect of Inter Miami CF's identity and mission. The club places a solid emphasis on interfacing with and contributing to the nearby community in Miami. By effectively locking in with the community, Inter Miami CF aims to make a positive and enduring effect past the soccer field. These endeavors not as it were to fortify the club's ties with its supporters but contribute to the general well-being and advancement of the neighborhood community. A few ways in which Inter Miami CF locks in with the community:

- Youth Advancement Programs:

Inter Miami CF contributes to youth advancement programs, advertising openings for youthful players to take part in soccer exercises, get coaching, and create their aptitudes. These programs aim to nurture neighborhood ability and make pathways for yearning for young players.

- Soccer Clinics and Camps:

The club organizes soccer clinics and camps for children in the community. These occasions give coaching, mentorship, and a chance for kids to experience the sport in a positive and strong environment.

- Community Outreach Activities:

Inter Miami CF engages in different outreach initiatives to positively impact the broader community. This may include participating in neighborhood occasions, supporting charitable causes, and collaborating with community organizations to address social issues.

- Instructive Programs:

The club may develop educational programs centered on advancing academic success, well-being and wellness, and life abilities among local youth. These programs point to back the all-encompassing advancement of young people.

- Player and Staff Inclusion:

Inter Miami

Players and staff from Inter Miami CF are regularly included in community activities. Whether it's going by schools, clinics, or community centers, their nearness serves to rouse and interface with fans and inhabitants.

- Community Associations:

Inter Miami CF builds up organizations with neighborhood businesses, organizations, and nonprofits. These associations make synergies that permit the club to use assets and bolster community initiatives effectively.

- Back for Neighborhood Causes:

The club may effectively bolster neighborhood causes and charities, using its stage to raise mindfulness and contribute to tending to issues such as instruction, well-being, and social balance.

- Fan Engagement Occasions:

Inter Miami CF organizes occasions to lock in straightforwardly with its fanbase. These occasions allow fans to connect with players, staff, and each other, cultivating a sense of community among supporters.

- Community-Driven Campaigns:

The club may dispatch campaigns that include the community, encouraging cooperation and . This could range from fan-driven initiatives to campaigns tending to particular community needs.

- Cultural Connections:

Inter Miami CF recognizes and celebrates the assorted social scene of Miami. The club may lock in activities that grasp the city's cultural richness, creating a sense of incorporation and solidarity.

6. Culture:

Inter Miami CF's culture is formed by The! different, energetic, and socially wealthy environment of Miami. The club aims to celebrate and coordinate these socials? components into its personality, making a one-of-a-kind and comprehensive involvement for players and supporters alike. As the club proceeds to advance, its culture will likely adjust and develop, affected by the dynamic nature of both Miami and the global soccer landscape. Inter Miami CF's culture may be a mix of the dynamic and differing impacts of Miami, the global nature of soccer, and the club's commitment to

community engagement. Whereas particular points of interest almost the culture may advance, these are key elements that contribute to Inter w CF's cultural identity:
Differing Qualities and Consideration:
Miami is known for its cultural diversity, with a dissolving pot of people from various backgrounds and ethnicities. Inter Miami CF embraces this diversity, fostering a comprehensive environment inside the club and among its fanbase.

- Expression: Aesthetic

Miami is famous for its vibrant craftsmanship scene, including street art, murals, and modern craftsmanship establishments. Inter Miami CF may draw inspiration from the city's aesthetic expression, consolidating components of imagination and visual request into its brand and activities.

- Music and Amusement:

Miami could be a center for music and excitement, especially impacted by Latin, Caribbean, and worldwide sounds. The club's occasions, celebrations, and matchday encounters may reflect the musical and exciting lavishness of the city.

- Fashion:

Miami is often related to a la mode and trendsetting culture. Inter Miami CF's branding, jerseys, and by and large tasteful may draw motivation from Miami's mold and plan patterns.

- Culinary Influences:

The differing culinary scene in Miami, featuring flavors from Latin America, the Caribbean, and beyond, may influence the club's events and associations. Inter Miami CF could collaborate with local culinary abilities to form unique fan encounters.

- Celebration of Legacy Months:

Inter Miami CF may engage in activities celebrating legacy months and social awareness, recognizing and honoring the commitments of various communities in Miami.

- Multilingual Communications:

Given the multilingual nature of Miami, Inter Miami CF may consolidate different dialects in its communications, recognizing English, Spanish, and other dialects spoken by the neighborhood populace.

- Community Engagement with Social Organizations:

The club may be accomplished with social organizations, celebrations, and occasions in Miami to effectively lock in with and back the social texture of the city.

- Association to Nearby Conventions:

Inter Miami CF may look to associate with and regard nearby conventions and traditions, making a sense of having a place for fans who recognize the social lavishness of Miami.

- Global Soccer Influence:

Soccer itself could be a worldwide wear with profound social roots. Inter Miami CF, as a soccer club, reflects the worldwide nature of the wear and the worldwide foundations of its players and fans.

2.1: The journey from dream to reality of Inter Miami

It could be a captivating account that includes assurance, challenges, and the realization of a vision. Here's an investigation of the key stages in this surprising travel. Inter Miami CF's travel is characterized by versatility, assurance, and a commitment to building a soccer bequest in Miami. As the club advances, each chapter includes the story of Inter Miami CF's commitment to the world of soccer and its effect on the nearby community. The journey from dream to reality for Inter Miami CF may be a confirmation of the control of vision, perseverance, and the significant effect that sports can have on a community. It could be a story that reverberates distance past the soccer pitch, capturing the creative ability of those who accept turning dreams into substantial, dynamic substances.

Imagining of Miami Soccer: Arrangement and Declaration (2014-2018): The beginning talks and desires were centered around not fair building up a soccer group but also making a social marvel that would reverberate with the different and dynamic city of Miami. The thought of bringing an MLS group to Miami was, to begin with, conceived when soccer symbol David Beckham worked out his alternative to claim an

MLS establishment. The travel started with plans for a team in Miami, but securing a reasonable stadium area was going to be a complex challenge that would reverberate with the differing and dynamic city of Miami.

Overcoming Obstacles: Battles and Lockhart Stadium (2018-2019) Changing the dream into reality was no simple assignment. The extent confronted various challenges, including securing reasonable arrival for a stadium, exploring bureaucratic obstacles, and picking up the community back. Overcoming these impediments required vital arranging, collaboration with nearby specialists, and a commitment to the long-term vision.

Assembling the Dream Group: The method of building the group went past the players on the field. It included collecting a dream group of financial specialists and pioneers who shared the vision and had the budgetary and vital insight to bolster the wander. The proprietorship gathers, including David Beckham and others, brought different mastery that would demonstrate vital in controlling the venture forward.

Disclosing the Personality: Branding and Peak Divulging (2018) The disclosing of Inter Miami's character was a pivotal step. The particular dark, pink, and white colors and the symbol highlighting two herons symbolized not as it were the club's commitment to the wear but also its association with the unique culture and soul of Miami. A Turning Point Accomplished: Inaugural Season (2020) The dream comes to an apex with Inter Miami CF making its big appearance in Major Inter Soccer. The inaugural season was not around soccer matches; it was a celebration of the realization of a vision that had been a long time in the making. Each amusement, each objective, and every interaction with the fans checked a critical step within the travel.

Community Connection: Community Engagement and Youth Improvement (Progressing) Necessarily to Inter Miami's journey was its commitment to interfacing with the community. The club started different programs, locked in in charity, and grasped the different social textures of Miami. This association not only fortified the bond between the group and its fans but also reflected the substance of the dream - to be an indispensable portion of Miami's personality.

Future Yearnings: Proceeded Development (Continuous) Whereas the dream has ended up a reality, Inter Miami's travel proceeds. Future yearnings incorporate the completion of Miami Flexibility Stop, the team's changeless domestic, and the interest in brilliance on the soccer field. The visionaries turned practitioners point for supported victory and a lasting legacy in the world of soccer and the Miami community.

2.2: Administration Experiences

It points to supply perusers with in-depth bits of knowledge about the people driving the victory and culture of Inter Miami CF, advertising a behind-the-scenes see of the administration that has been instrumental in forming the club's trajectory. The Substance of Administration in Sports is building up the centrality of authority inside a sports organization like

Inter Miami CF, setting the Organize and looking into the impact of key officials and coaching staff on the club's travel.

Profiles of Key Officials

Jorge Mas - Overseeing Owner
 Foundation and Vision: A see into Jorge Mas's foundation and the vision he brought to Inter Miami CF. Understanding his part in major choices and methodologies.
Paul McDonough - Chief Soccer Officer and Donning Chief: Diving into his techniques for player enlistment and advancement. Analyzing his commitments to forming the donning heading of the club.
Chris Allan - Chief Lawful Officer: Investigating the lawful viewpoints and challenges confronted by Inter Miami CF. Enumerating Allan's part in guaranteeing legitimate compliance.
Jurgen Mainka - Chief Business Officer: Analyzing his effect on the club's commerce site and brand. Talking

about activities to lock in with the nearby and worldwide community.

Kurt Schmid - Specialized Executive: Detailing Schmid's part in forming the technical direction of the group. Highlighting activities for sustaining young talent in the youth foundation.

Elements of the Coaching Staff

Phil Neville - Head Coach: Understanding Neville's coaching logic and fashion. Experiences into his approach to overseeing and persuading players.

Examining the roles of collaborator coaches, counting Jason Kreis and Anthony Pulis.

Bolster Staff: Goalkeeper Coach, Fitness Coach, Execution Examiner: Displaying the commitments of different back staff individuals.

Decision-Making

Investigating occurrences where authority confronted challenges and the decision-making forms attempted. Emphasizing the importance of a bound-together administration approach amid basic junctures. Building a Feasible Culture, talks about how authority cultivates a positive and sustainable organizational culture.Highlighting activities to advance collaboration and compelling communication.Investigating the administration team's goals for a long time. Talking about how the authority envisions adjusting to future challenges and openings.

CHAPTER 3: RISING FROM THE MARSHES

Muddy waters at the start, When the club took its first steps, the waters in which it sailed were full of uncertainty. The challenges during training were not always clear-cut, and leaders had to navigate the murky landscape of decision-making, financial considerations, and strategic planning. In the darkness, Inter Miami CF's resilience emerged as a guiding light as setbacks and obstacles were opportunities for the club to demonstrate perseverance. From financial hurdles to securing a home venue, we met every challenge with the spirit of resilience that has formed the basis of the club's identity. Inter Miami CF has learned to adapt and grow in the face of uncertainty. Early setbacks provided fertile ground for the deep roots of resilience, ensuring the club's survival and eventual victory. Building team unity in turbulent times: Just as a swamp requires a complex network to thrive, Inter Miami CF fosters team unity in turbulent times. This encapsulates Inter Miami CF's transformation journey, highlighting its ability to overcome challenges and adapt to its environment, bounce back, and become an established force in the world of football. The Swamp represents the first challenges faced when the club was founded and reflects the uncertainties and obstacles that had to be overcome. The complexities of starting a new football club in a competitive environment, the club overcame its initial challenges while maintaining its vision of building a successful and influential football franchise because this book captures the essence of the resilience, vision, and adaptability that characterized Inter Miami CF's early journey. The murky waters of the swamp metaphorically represent the early struggles and challenges faced by Inter Miami CF which emphasizes the club's resilience and shows how it emerged from the metaphorical darkness stronger and more determined. Like the resilient flora of wetlands, we have learned to adapt to the challenges of competition and form cohesive units that weather storms together. Symbolic Darkness is more than a challenge and embodies the essence of the club's transformation journey. There are opportunities for growth, resilience, and the emergence of stronger companies amidst uncertainty which reflects the club's efforts to build a strong foundation early on and create stability despite the unstable ground. Inter Miami CF's early years were characterized by the challenge of creating stability on surfaces that seemed inherently unstable.

Inter Miami CF faced financial challenges with its new venture, but through financial responsibility and strategic financial management, the club was able to weather the economic uncertainty and position itself strongly for future growth. We were able to establish a financial foundation and build a foundation as Inter Miami CF actively collaborated with South Florida and developed a symbiotic relationship. The support of the local community has become a stabilizing force and strengthened the club's roots in the region. The selection and development of DRV PNK Stadium as the home stadium was a pivotal moment in creating stability. The symbolism of the purpose-built stadium cemented the club's presence and provided a secure anchor for players, fans, and the organization. The swamp symbolizes South

Inter Miami

Florida's rich diversity and reflects the club's embrace of the region's unique cultural landscape into its identity and values. Along the way, Inter Miami CF has demonstrated the ability to turn challenges into opportunities, adapt strategies, and learn from setbacks. The choice of DRV PNK Stadium represents a highlight of the journey, comparable to the creation of a new landscape emerging from the swamp. The transition to stability and growth symbolizes the club's gradual transition from a state of swamp instability to a more stable and established state. Inter Miami CF's journey is one of growth, development, and establishing a strong presence in the world of football. A legacy of resilience and winning: Rising from the Swamp contributes to Inter Miami CF's enduring legacy and demonstrates the club's ability to overcome challenges and leave a lasting impression which is victory over adversity and defines the early story of Inter Miami CF. Just as a wetland evolves, Inter Miami CF will continue to evolve, adapt, and grow as conditions change. Looking forward, creating a sense of anticipation as the club continues its journey beyond the swamp.

3.1: Connecting with South Florida's Rich Ecosystem

In vibrant South Florida, Inter Miami CF wanted to not only establish itself as a soccer club but also establish a deep connection with the region's rich and diverse ecosystem. This chapter examines how the club's history is intertwined with the unique cultural, environmental, and social elements that define South Florida.

 Embracing Cultural Diversity: At the heart of Inter Miami CF's connection to South Florida has been an embrace of cultural diversity. The region's multicultural landscape became an integral part of the club's identity and was reflected in its values, public relations, and engagement strategies and examines how Inter Miami CF celebrates and integrates South Florida's diverse cultural elements.

 Heron Symbolism: Central to the Club's identity was the symbolism of the Heron. Native to South Florida, the heron has become a symbol of Inter Miami CF's connection to the local ecosystem which explores the importance of herons, how they represent the region's unique fauna, and the role they play in shaping the club's visual identity.

Celebrating South Florida's Heritage: In Miami CF actively participates in efforts to celebrate South Florida's heritage. From collaborating with local artists to hosting events that showcase the region's rich history, the club strived to connect with the community on a cultural level. Beyond cultural ties, Inter Miami CF has taken steps to help protect South Florida's natural environment and efforts related to environmental management, sustainability, and community greening projects. It details the club's commitment to being a responsible and environmentally conscious organization within its ecosystem.

Community Integration Program: Connecting with South Florida's rich ecosystem required direct community engagement. Inter Miami CF has launched a program targeting local neighborhoods, schools, and organizations. It describes regional integration efforts and shows how clubs became active and active participants in the social fabric of their regions.

Visual Representation in Branding: The club's visual branding played an important role in symbolizing its connection to South Florida's rich ecosystem. The visual elements of a club's crest, colors, and general branding consider how these elements visually convey a deep connection to the local environment.

Supporter Involvement and Local Pride: Strong ties to South Florida resonate with supporters. Inter Miami CF's involvement with the region fostered local pride among its fans. We explore fan engagement strategies that have strengthened the bond between clubs and their passionate fan bases.

CHAPTER 4: FORGING A LEGACY ON FOREIGN SOIL

In the larger fabric of soccer culture, a team's journey extends far beyond the confines of its home stadium. Away games are more than just a competition of skill. It's a journey into uncharted territory, a pilgrimage for passionate fans to carry the club's soul to faraway lands. In the following pages, we will unravel the chapter of Inter Miami CF's glorious story entitled "Creating a presence outside his home stadium". As the sun sets on a familiar pitch, Inter Miami's 12th man emerges from the shadows and transforms every away game of his into a spectacle of unyielding passion. Away cheers, chants, and a symphony of pink and black seas paint overseas stadiums in the colors of Miami. It's a journey marked by iconic moments, resilient performances, and connections that transcend geographic boundaries. This chapter delves into his experience with Inter Miami away from home, examining the complexities of travel support, the challenges of being on the road, and the indelible impact he had on players and his community of world football. From memorable victories to rituals that unite fans, we tell the story of a club that has made an unmistakable mark on the world stage, beyond the pitch. Join the chants that echo through arenas abroad, the camaraderie born of shared victories and defeats, and the indomitable spirit that drives Inter Miami CF beyond its home stadium. This is a story that transcends boundaries and is a testament to the lasting legacy left by the club's loyal fans, who strive for victory. The great symphony of football, where every note played during a match echoes, has a unique melody composed by the 12th man on the street. As the pink and black supporters embark on a journey to a foreign land, their significance goes beyond the cheers that echo in the away stands, becoming the heartbeat of Inter's Miami CF and injecting a vital passion that pulses through the team's veins and explores the diverse faces and journeys of Inter Miami's traveling fans, we hope to recognize the unique role they play in emotionally building team morale. They are an invisible force powered by passion, determination, and unity within the team, turning every away game into a canvas on which the art of football is painted with the brush of collective belief. Its importance goes beyond the cheers echoing in the away stands which becomes the very heartbeat of Inter Miami CF and injects a vital passion that pulses through the team's veins.

Unwavering support: An away game is more than just a match played on an unfamiliar pitch. It is a battlefield where the 12th man transforms into an indomitable force. Their presence, resembling a sea of pink and black, constantly reminds players that they are not alone in their quest for victory. It is the support that transcends the boundaries of geographical distance and a collective voice that resonates despite the disadvantages of a foreign land.

Ignite the Spirit: Street's unique role as his 12th man lies in his ability to ignite the team's spirit. When the players step onto the away pitch, the cheers of the away fans become a rallying cry and give the team even more determination. Cheers, chants, and unwavering support ring in the ears of every player, serving as a catalyst that boosts team morale and pushes them to achieve their best.

 Foreign Face: In a sea of contrasting colors, the twelfth man stands out as a familiar face in a foreign land. The importance of their presence is not lost on the players, who see prominent banners, and chants that reflect their names, and every tackle, every run, every goal has a piece of Miami on their side. I'm inspired by things that visually remind me of something.

 Emotional Fuel: Beyond tactical maneuvers and strategic plays, the 12th man's impact on team morale is emotional. Players feed off the emotional fuel that traveling fans provide the elation of shared joy and the calm of a collective embrace of unwavering loyalty. The 12th man on the street is not just a bystander, they are emotional partners on the roller coaster that is the game of football exploring the diverse faces and journeys of Inter Miami's traveling fans. We must recognize the unique role they play as emotional builders of team morale. They are an invisible force powered by passion, determination, and unity within the team, turning every away game into a canvas on which the art of football is painted with the brush of collective belief.

 Setting the stage for the away fan experience: In the vibrant world of soccer, where the cheers of fans echo through stadiums, there are unique stories that unfold beyond the familiar embrace of home turf. This is the chapter in which the Inter Miami CF story takes a transformative leap forward. It's the story of his 12th man on the street, a passionate adventure that adds another layer to the club's identity. The fans' away experience, a symphony of passion in overseas arenas, plays an important role in the grand theater of Inter Miami's journey. Beyond score lines and wins, the away fan experience embodies the heartbeat of Inter Miami CF. It's a story that goes to the heart of the club's identity, as the Pink and Black faithful travel across the country to rub shoulders with their teams, their importance is felt beyond their playing time. Your presence is more than just a cheering choir, it is a testament to the unwavering commitment of a community united by a shared love of the game and an unwavering belief in the club.

Uncharted territory: Away games are the canvas on which Inter Miami's character is painted in vibrant colors. The importance of these encounters lies not only in the results on the field, but also in the collective energy, shared rituals, and formation of unbreakable bonds. The experience for away fans is an expedition into uncharted territory, where every chant, every flag, and every celebration is a stroke of emphasis on Inter Miami's identity.

In The Shadow Of A Foreign Arena: As the club begins its journey from the sunny shores of Miami, the traveling fans become the torchbearers of Inter Miami's spirit. Its importance is not limited to his 90 minutes of the match, it extends to the stories they tell, the traditions they uphold, and the fortitude they bring to the stands. The story of Inter Miami goes beyond the experience of away fans and leaves an indelible mark on the collective memory of football lovers around the world. The stage is set for an exploration into the diverse faces, the heartfelt stories, and the enduring impact of Inter Miami's 12th Man on the road, the narrative that defines the club's journey from vision to victory.

4.1: Detailing the Rituals and Traditions

Sometime recently the Pink and Dark reliably set foot on the new landscape of an absent coordinate, an embroidered artwork of customs and conventions is fastidiously woven, making a canvas that captures the substance of their unflinching dedication. This chapter digs into the prologue of Inter Miami's absent journey, investigating the traditions that shape the collective character of the traveling fans and produce the bonds that carry them through the trip.

1. The Gathering: Detail the pre-trip get-togethers where fans come together to construct camaraderie and share expectations. Investigate how these social occasions serve as a stage for arranging coordination, trading stories, and cultivating a sense of community.

2. The Chants and Cheers Practice: Reveal the practices of chants, cheers, and melodies that will resound through the absent stands. Highlighting the part of these practices in joining together the fanbase and planning them to form a climate of domestic absence from domestic.

3. Tifo and Standard Creation: Give experiences in the creation of tifos, standards, and visual shows that will gladly speak to Inter Miami. Investigating the collaborative endeavors and aesthetic expressions of fans as they create images of the bolster.

4. Away-Day Clothing: Exhibiting the fastidious choice of clothing that fans consider for absent trips. Talking about the importance of wearing particular colors, shirts, or adornments that symbolize solidarity and character.

5. Traveling Conventions: Investigating one-of-a-kind customs related to the travel itself, such as particular travel courses, pre-match pitstops, or notorious points of interest going to the traveling fans. Highlighting how these conventions contribute to the sense of enterprise and expectation.

6. Sharing Stories and Superstitions: Jumping into the convention of sharing accounts, vital absent encounters,

and superstitions among fans. Outlining how these stories got to be a portion of the texture that ties the fanbase together.

7. Community Commitments: Grandstand community-driven activities or charity occasions organized by fans sometime recently setting out on absent trips. Looking at how these commitments increase the positive effect of the fanbase past the boundaries of the soccer field.

8. Culinary Culture: Investigating any culinary ceremonies related to absent trips, such as particular nourishments or drinks that fans enjoy to form a shared encounter, and how these culinary conventions contribute to the tactile embroidered artwork of absent days.

9. Flight Ceremonies: Detailing any flight ceremonies or send-offs organized by the nearby fan community to offer goodbye to the traveling supporters. Capture the passionate minutes as fans plan to set out on the absent travel and by unraveling these ceremonies and conventions, we pick up a more profound understanding of the social texture that wraps Inter Miami's traveling

fans. Each custom may be a brushstroke on the canvas of their collective character, building a story that rises above the miles traveled and changes absent trips into cherished chapters of the Pink and Dark chronicles.

CHAPTER 5: FUTURE HORIZONS

As Inter Miami CF looks to long-standing time, the chapter investigates the fragile move between the ageless conventions that shape the club's wealthy history and the imaginative techniques that will move it into unused wildernesses. This chapter envisions the way forward, exploring the fine line between honoring the bequest and grasping the progressions that will characterize Connect Miami's story. Long-run calls for Inter Miami CF, and at its center lies a fragile move between the cherished conventions that characterize its personality and the tireless interest of advancement into the club's journey of exploring future skylines, keeping up an adjustment that regards its legacy while grasping the conceivable outcomes of tomorrow.

Protecting Establishing Values:

Inter Miami

As Inter Miami CF looks ahead, protecting its establishing values gets to be foremost. How the club plans to maintain the center standards and vision that set its course, guaranteeing that the substance of its character remains intact through advancing seasons. Inter Miami CF was born from a vision that rose above ordinary standards. This portion of the area returns to the visionary beginning of the club, highlighting the center values and desires that fueled its creation. It digs into how these starting values proceed to shape the club's direction. At the heart of Connect Miami CF's establishing values could be a profound commitment to the community it calls domestic. This segment investigates the club's progressing endeavors to lock in with and contribute emphatically to the South Florida community. From grassroots activities to community outreach programs, Inter Miami CF proceeds to maintain its commitment to making a significant effect. Grasping differences is more than a buzzword for Inter Miami CF, it's an essential esteem that shapes the club's character. The club effectively grasps differences in all its shapes, from social foundations to fan encounters. It investigates how Inter Miami CF's commitment to differing qualities enhances not as it were the soccer pitch but the broader community. Protecting establishing values includes sustaining the following era of ability such as youth advancement, and displaying how the club's foundation programs and activities contribute to building an enduring bequest. It highlights the significance of ingraining core values in youthful players who speak to the club. Values are not fair words, they are epitomized in activities and administration. Inter Miami CF keeps up consistency in leadership, guaranteeing that the directing standards set forward by the authors stay at the forefront of decision-making. It emphasizes the part of administration in protecting the club's character, the conservation of establishing values is interlaced with the club's social integration and imagery and leverages social components, symbols, and ceremonies to fortify its character. From the herons that take off amid key minutes to the imagery inserted within the peak, the club's social integration serves as a capable confirmation of its values. Open communication and fan engagement are columns of Connect Miami CF's values.

Inter Miami

The club's commitment to straightforwardness with its supporters, cultivating a sense of consideration and shared reason,and investigating how fan criticism and engagement contribute to the ceaseless advancement of Inter Miami. Protecting establishing values rises above the boundaries of the soccer pitch. Inter Miami CF envisions clearing out an enduring bequest past the domain of sports—a bequest that adjusts with the values upon which the club was built. It investigates activities that contribute to the persevering effect of Inter Miami CF within the broader setting of South Florida.

Inventive Player Development:
The long run of Inter Miami CF includes supporting ability and advancing player advancement methodologies. The club envisions inventive approaches to scouting, preparing, and fostering youthful ability while remaining true to the ethos of its soccer foundation. Within the dynamic world of soccer, player development isn't almost the show, it's almost making a pipeline for the longer term. Inter Miami CF's commitment to imaginative player improvement,

exhibits the club's forward-thinking procedures in scouting, preparing, and cultivating the development of youthful ability. The travel starts with a sharp eye for ability and grasped imaginative scouting techniques to distinguish promising players from assorted foundations. From worldwide scouting systems to leveraging advanced information analytics, the club is at the bleeding edge of distinguishing the stars of tomorrow. Beyond identification, Inter Miami CF features an unmistakable youth improvement logic to sustaining youthful ability, emphasizing not fair specialized abilities but moreover ingrains center values that adjust with the club's character. It investigates how the youth institute serves as a breeding ground for future stars. Innovation is at the heart of preparing techniques at Inter Miami CF. This portion of the segment exhibits how the club leverages cutting-edge innovation in preparing sessions. From virtual reality recreations to data-driven execution examination, players experience preparing encounters that are not as thorough but also custom-fitted to the person's needs. The science behind player development is ever-evolving, and Inter Miami CF remains ahead of the curve. From harm avoidance to optimizing execution through sustenance and recuperation, the club's commitment to an all-encompassing approach is clear in its imaginative methodologies. Inventive player advancement amplifies past the physical domain to mental conditioning. Inter Miami CF prioritizes mental versatility and cognitive advancement from mindfulness preparing to sports brain research bolster, players are prepared to explore the mental challenges of proficient soccer. Within the imaginative biological system of player development, Inter Miami CF has set up clear pathways to the primary group. Youthful gifts advance through the ranks, benefiting from a consistent move that adjusts with the club's general playing reasoning and highlights victory stories of players who have risen through the ranks. Inter Miami CF's commitment to advancement amplifies universally and builds up associations and trades with universal institutes and clubs. By uncovering youthful abilities to assorted playing styles and situations, the club improves their travel. Advancement in player development also includes mentorship and facilitates mentorship programs, where prepared players direct and rouse the next generation. The accentuation is not as it were on aptitude exchange but too on ingrains a solid sense of camaraderie inside the Inter Miami CF family.

Stadium Improvements and Innovative Integration: As DRV PNK Stadium stands as an image of Inter Miami CF's domestic, the club looks towards imaginative stadium improvements and innovative integration and plans for making an immersive matchday involvement through innovation regarding the memorable and social centrality of the setting. The soul of soccer is not limited to the pitch, it resounds all through the stadium. This segment plunges into how Inter Miami CF is at the forefront of stadium improvements and innovative integration, changing DRV PNK Stadium into a center of advancement that elevates fan involvement and operational productivity. The pulse of DRV PNK Stadium is its matchday air, and innovative integration plays a key role in making it an immersive involvement. Inter Miami CF employs cutting-edge innovation to upgrade fan engagement, from intelligent shows to increased reality components that bring the matchday display to life. Technological integration extends to the very seats fans possess and leverages smart seating innovation to enhance ticketing preparation. From versatile ticketing to personalized fan encounters based on situate area, the club guarantees that each perspective of the fan's travel is seamless and helpful. Stadium improvements go past the stands. Inter Miami CF has made high-tech fan zones inside DRV PNK Stadium from intuitive shows celebrating the club's history to increased reality establishments that lock in fans of all ages, these zones include an additional layer of excitement to the by and large matchday experience. Within the computerized age, connectivity is fundamental, so investing in a state-of-the-art foundation to supply fans with an upgraded network throughout DRV PNK Stadium. From high-speed Wi-Fi to devoted versatile apps, the club guarantees that fans remain consistently associated with the activity on and off the field. For the tech-savvy soccer devotees, Inter Miami CF introduces expanded reality coordinate bits of knowledge. Players bits of knowledge, and strategic investigation, including a modern measurement to their understanding of the diversion. Advancement in stadium enhancements also means reaching fans past the physical limits of the stadium. Inter Miami CF grasps virtual fan engagement through live gushing, virtual observer parties, and intuitively online communities that interface with fans universally, making a joined-together front supporting the club. The stadium encounter is fragmented without reveling in culinary delights and civilities and coordinating innovation into concessions and conveniences. From portable requests to cashless exchanges, the club guarantees that fans appreciate a streamlined and tech-savvy involvement. Stadium upgrades to adjust with Inter Miami CF's commitment to environmental sustainability. This section talks about how the club coordinates eco-friendly technologies and jones, such as energy-efficient lighting and waste reduction measures, making DRV PNK Stadium a demonstration for green sports offices. In past fan encounters, innovative integration enhances operational effectiveness, using technology to streamline stadium operations, from upkeep assignments to security protocols, ensuring that the behind-the-scenes endeavors contribute to a consistent and secure matchday. Advancement of Fan Engagement: Long-run skylines of Inter Miami CF extend to its fanbase. Imaginative fan engagement strategies, from intuitively digital experiences to community outreach activities, maintain the pulse of Inter Miami CF amplifies past the pitch to the energetic supporters who bring the stadium to life. Inter Miami CF has ceaselessly improved to associate with its different and intense fanbase. The travel starts with the establishing fanbase that laid the basis for a soccer culture in South Florida, the early days were supporters joined together beneath the banner of Inter Miami CF, cultivating a sense of community and shared excitement for the club's beginning with the advanced age came the advancement of fan communities. Online stages and social media to put through with supporters all-inclusive from official fan gatherings to intuitive social media campaigns, the club has fostered a virtual community where fans share their enthusiasm for the team. The advancement of fan engagement rises above the boundaries of the stadium. Inter Miami CF has changed matchday encounters into intelligent displays from live surveys and interactive challenges amid matches to locks in halftime shows, the club keeps supporters effectively included indeed when miles are absent from the stadium. Inter Miami CF recognizes the power of fan-driven activities. Engages supporters to require the lead in organizing occasions, making traditions, and contributing to the overall fan encounter. The advancement of fan engagement includes giving supporters a stage to shape the character of the club. In reaction to worldwide shifts, Inter Miami CF has spearheaded virtual observation parties. Utilizing video conferencing and streaming stages to make virtual spaces where fans can interface, celebrate objectives, and share the highs and lows of the amusement, cultivating a sense of camaraderie. While innovation interfaces fans all-inclusive, in-stadium engagement remains a cornerstone. Advanced in-stadium encounters, consolidating intelligently shows, fan zones, and halftime shows that charm the attention of supporters and make enduring recollections inside DRV PNK Stadium. The advancement of fan engagement expands intelligence with players and encourages player engagement with the community. From signature sessions to community occasions, the club guarantees that supporters have openings to associate with the players they enthusiastically bolster. Inter Miami CF values supporter input and output, where fans can contribute thoughts, voice concerns, and effectively take an interest in forming the club's course. The advancement includes a complementary relationship where the club tunes in, adjusts, and advances based on the priceless input from its supporters. The advancement of fan engagement is a continuous journey. Examining how Inter Miami CF envisions presenting modern and imaginative fan engagement activities from increased reality encounters to personalized content delivery, the club remains committed to remaining ahead of the bend.

Versatile Strategic Procedures:
On the field, long-term includes versatile strategic techniques and gameplay advancements. Inter Miami CF plans to adjust the immortal standards of excellent amusement with cutting-edge strategies and techniques

that keep the club competitive in an energetic soccer scene. Within the ever-evolving world of soccer, the capacity to adjust on the field may be a trademark of victory. The versatile strategic methodologies utilized by Inter Miami CF, showcase how the club navigates the energetic scene of soccer, altering its approach to different challenges and rivals. At the center of versatile strategic methodologies lies a logic of adaptability, Inter Miami CF grasps the concept of strategic flexibility, emphasizing the significance of flexibility in both hostile and cautious scenarios. One of the key components of versatile strategies is the smoothness of arrangements. Inter Miami CF's playing style isn't kept to an inflexible structure but or maybe advance based on the qualities of the squad, rival examination, and situational requests. The club grasps arrangements that give a strong establishment while permitting energetic alterations amid the match, adaptation starts with an intensive understanding of the adversary and taking an opponent-centric approach to strategic arranging. Through in-depth investigation and vital planning, the club tailors its strategies to misuse shortcomings and capitalize on openings displayed by specific enemies. The magnificence of versatile strategies is uncovered within the capacity to create real-time adjustments during matches. Driven by the head coach, who screens the stream of the diversion and executes strategic changes on the fly from substitutions to positional tweaks, the club remains dexterous to reply to unfurling flow. Adjustment expands to cautious techniques, counting squeezing and protective varieties, diverse squeezing styles, and cautious setups based on the particular necessities of the amusement from high-intensity squeezing to organized protective structures, the club's cautious strategies are formed by the context of the match and adaptive tactics moreover envelop set-piece play. Both unpalatable and protectively, as vital minutes inside a coordinate, the club's approach to set pieces is energetic, with varieties custom-made to misuse the shortcomings of opponents or capitalize on particular player qualities, players are key performing artists within the execution of strategic procedures. The flexibility of players and their capacity to perform in numerous positions contribute to the general versatile nature of the club's strategic approach. Versatile strategies require continuous training and examination. Inter Miami CF contributes to progress preparation sessions and video examinations to strengthen versatile strategic standards. The club's commitment to player improvement amplifies strategic mindfulness and the ability to execute differing procedures. Versatile strategies moreover expand to squad revolution and administration. Deliberately pivots players, oversees workloads, and guarantees that the squad is prepared to handle the requests of a stuffed installation plan. This versatile approach points to maximizing player execution and minimizing the hazard of wounds.

Social Integration:
As the club evolves, cultural integration remains a driving constraint, Inter Miami CF Proceeded envisions weaving more profound strings into the social texture of South Florida, grasping differences, and advancing to be a reflection of the wealthy embroidered artwork that characterizes the region. Diversity is the pulse of South

Inter Miami

Florida, and at the center of Inter Miami CF's personality may be a commitment to proceed social integration. The rich embroidered artwork of societies defines the locale, cultivating an environment where soccer becomes a binding together drive that rises above borders. The mosaic of South Florida may be a kaleidoscope of societies, dialects, and conventions. Inter Miami CF recognizes and celebrates this diversity, weaving it into the exceptional texture of the club, the dynamic neighborhoods to the worldwide fanbase, the club stands as a reflection of the unique blend that characterizes South Florida. Dialect could be a bridge that interfaces communities, and Inter Miami CF communicates within the dialects spoken by its diverse fanbase. The club utilizes multilingual communication over different stages, guaranteeing that supporters from diverse etymological foundations feel not as if they were invited but completely locked in with the club's account. Social integration goes past the stadium dividers, this actively engages in community outreach programs that reflect the differing needs and interface of South Florida, soccer clinics in socially wealthy neighborhoods to instructive activities, and the club gets to be an indispensable portion of the communities it serves. Inter Miami CF transforms coordinate days into cultural celebrations, the club joins social legacy celebrations into its occasions from themed coordinate days to collaborative activities with cultural organizations, and the club gives a platform for diverse communities to grandstand their traditions and contribute to the general matchday experience. The commitment to social integration is reflected within the leadership of Inter Miami CF, the club values differences in its administration group, guaranteeing that voices from different foundations contribute to the decision-making forms. The comprehensive administration demonstration strengthens the club's association with its diverse fanbase. Cultural integration may be a collaborative exertion, and Inter Miami CF engages its supporters to require the lead, support bunches speaking to distinctive communities to collaborative occasions, the club's supporters effectively shape the social account of Inter Miami CF. The players on the field speak to a worldwide embroidered artwork of ability Inter Miami CF's list incorporates players from different worldwide foundations. The club's commitment to scouting and selecting players from different districts contributes not as it were to on-field victory but moreover to the socially differing qualities that define the squad. Inter Miami CF's fan engagement expands to all-inclusive, and the club cultivates associations with supporters around the world creating a worldwide Inter Miami CF family. From international watch parties to virtual fan events, the club guarantees that its worldwide fanbase is a necessary portion of the cultural integration account. Social integration involves education and mindfulness. Inter Miami CF builds up instructive organizations to advance social understanding, collaborations with schools to activities that highlight the commitments of distinctive societies, the club becomes a catalyst for social instruction in South Florida.

Maintainable and Responsible Operations:
Looking to the future includes a commitment to maintainability and mindful operations. This area investigates how Inter Miami CF aims to minimize its

ecological footprint, embracing eco-friendly activities, and contributing emphatically to the communities it serves. Inter Miami CF recognizes its obligation to not as it were to engage on the pitch but also to contribute emphatically to the environment and community. This area dives into how the club has embraced sustainable and dependable operations, committing to support both the excellent diversion and the world in which it unfurls. At the heart of maintainable operations is DRV PNK Stadium, the home of Inter Miami CF. This portion of the section investigates the green initiatives actualized at the stadium. From energy-efficient lighting to water preservation measures, the club is devoted to minimizing its environmental impression and making an economical matchday encounter. A shining case of maintainability is the integration of sun-oriented vitality at DRV PNK Stadium. How Inter Miami CF tackles the control of the sun to create clean and renewable vitality. The club's commitment to sun-based vitality adjusts with its vision for a greener and more sustainable future. The commitment to responsible operations expands to squander reduction. Inter Miami CF actualizes techniques to play down squander generation during matches and occasions. From reusing activities to organizations with eco-friendly vendors, the club endeavors to form a waste-conscious environment. Maintainable operations too include reexamining transportation and advancing eco-friendly transportation activities for fans attending matches. From empowering open transportation to giving bicycle racks and electric vehicle charging stations, the club aims to decrease the natural effect of matchday travel. Past the stadium gates, Inter Miami CF contributes to making green spaces within the community. This portion of the area investigates how the club underpins and starts ventures that upgrade open spaces, promoting natural supportability and community well-being. From tree-planting initiatives to stop beautification projects, the club points to a positive effect. Inter Miami CF recognizes the significance of educating another era about environmental duty. The club engages in youth natural instruction programs. Collaborations with schools, natural workshops, and activities that rouse youthful minds to be stewards of the planet contribute to the club's broader mission. Sustainability amplifies the merchandise that fans wear with pride. Inter Miami CF joins economical homes within the creation of club stock and apparel. From utilizing eco-friendly materials to implementing moral sourcing homes, the club guarantees that the Inter Miami CF brand adjusts with dependable buyer choices. Taking responsibility for its carbon impression, Inter Miami CF locks in carbon-balanced activities. The club contributes to ventures that offset its carbon emanations, contributing to natural preservation and feasible advancement. The commitment to carbon nonpartisanship reflects the club's dedication to capable operations. Straightforwardness and responsibility are indispensable to responsible operations. Inter Miami CF communicates its maintainability endeavors to the open from yearly maintainability reports to locks in with fans on natural initiatives, the club illustrates its commitment to being accountable for its natural effect. Supportability could be a journey of continuous improvement. Emphasizing how Inter Miami CF remains committed to advancement in maintainable and mindful operations. The club grasps unused advances, investigates imaginative arrangements, and advances its hones to contribute genuinely to a sustainable and flourishing future.

Developing Conventions:

Within the sensitive adjustment between convention and development, the plausibility of modern ceremonies and conventions developing the club expects the natural improvement of customs that reverberate with future eras, contributing to the advancing story of Inter Miami CF. Conventions are the strings that weave the texture of a club's personality, and at Inter Miami CF, the travel incorporates the creation of modern conventions that resonate with supporters. The interesting social embroidered artwork of Inter Miami CF. Conventions regularly start with shared encounters that take off an enduring effect and how Inter Miami CF leverages key minutes, both on and off the pitch, to construct associations with supporters. Turning point victory to community initiatives, the club looks to form shared encounters that lay the establishment for developing conventions. Matchdays are a canvas for the convention, and Inter Miami CF portrays a picture of inclusivity. The club is cultivating comprehensive matchday customs that join together supporters from pre-match ceremonies that celebrate differences to post-match conventions that symbolize solidarity. Inter Miami CF points to form a matchday involvement that resounds with fans of all foundations. Conventions frequently arise naturally from the enthusiasm of the supporters energize and grasp supporter-initiated conventions, chants that resound through DRV PNK Stadium to supporter-led occasions that become yearly installations, the club recognizes the noteworthiness of conventions born from the fanbase. Inter Miami CF effectively collaborates with different social organizations to enhance its conventions. The club locks in associations with social bunches, cultivating collaborations that bring interesting conventions and celebrations to matchdays. The integration of social components includes profundity to the rising conventions of Inter Miami CF, the club peak and colors serve as a canvas for imagery and convention and infuse meaning into its visual character, making an establishment for emerging traditions. From the herons within the peak to the centrality of pink and dark, each component tells a story that fans can carry forward. Rising conventions contribute to the bequest of a club and its purposefulness around legacy-building activities. From time capsules to commemorative occasions, the club actively involves supporters in initiatives that lay the foundation for conventions that will be cherished for eras. Conventions amplify past the stadium into the community and how Inter Miami CF organizes community association occasions that have become necessary to the club's conventions. From neighborhood celebrations to community outreach programs, the club guarantees that its conventions reverberate distant past the pitch within the computerized age, conventions discover modern expressions. Inter Miami CF is grasping intuitively advanced conventions that interface supporters online, from computerized matchday ceremonies to intuitive social media campaigns, the club leverages innovation to make conventions that bridge the crevice between physical and virtual communities. Conventions, whereas established in history, are versatile to changing times. Inter Miami CF navigates advancing scenes, guaranteeing that developing conventions stay significant and resonate with modern eras of supporters. The club's commitment to versatile conventions reflects a forward-thinking approach.

CONCLUSION

From Vision to Victory, we discover ourselves submerged within the wealthy embroidered artwork of a club that has risen above simple presence on the soccer pitch. The pages of this chronicle disclose a story that goes past triumphs and routes, typifying the pitch of Inter Miami CF's momentous travel.

From the introductory vision that started the creation of this soccer sensation, we have seen the fastidious weaving of dreams into reality. The establishment laid by the club's authors, pervaded with enthusiasm and prescience, has gotten to be the bedrock upon which triumphs and challenges alike have been met.

The account strings complicatedly through the foundation of a one-of-a-kind character, where the notorious pink and dark tones symbolize not as if they were a group but a community. The herons in flight inside the peak ended up more than an image; they epitomized the taking off the soul of a club coming to unused statues.

Inter Miami

All through these pages, the peruser has been an indispensable portion of the Inter Miami CF family, feeling the beat of matchdays at DRV PNK Stadium, celebrating shared victories, and weathering the storms of overcome together. The rise of modern conventions and the continuation of immortal customs serve as a confirmation of the solidarity produced inside the different and energetic fanbase.

The administration group, coaching staff, and players have carved their stories into the chronicles of Inter Miami CF's history. From versatile strategic methodologies on the field to supporting developing abilities through imaginative player advancement, each chapter divulges the devotion and flexibility that characterize the ethos of the club.

However, this chronicle isn't an inactive memory of occasions; it's a living confirmation of flexibility and persistent advancement. As we explore the questionable territory, rise from the bogs, and manufacture a character that resounds with South Florida's wealthy biological system, Inter Miami CF develops not just as a soccer club but as an energetic drive interlaced with the soul of its environment.

The commitment to maintainability, capable operations, and the producing of associations inside the community exhibit a club careful of its impact past the ultimate shriek. It could be a testament to a vision that amplifies past the boundaries of the soccer pitch, weaving Inter Miami CF into the exceptional texture of South Florida's socially embroidered artwork.

From the visionary initiation to the show victory, Inter Miami Chronicles calls us to reflect on a journey that encapsulates versatility, differences, and the unflinching interest in greatness. The rising from the swamps gets to be an allegory not fair for the club's climb but for the collective soul that propels it forward.

As we near this chapter of the Inter Miami Chronicles, we are cleared out with a sense of triumph and the expectation of what the long-term holds. The street to victory is one cleared with energy, solidarity, and a commitment to standards that rise above the wear itself. May this chronicle not as it were a record of the past but a source of motivation for the chapters however to be composed. As Inter Miami CF proceeds its travel, the echoes of victory past propel the club toward modern skylines, where the vision gets to be an ever-evolving reality, and victory is celebrated not as endpoints but as breakthroughs on an eternal journey for triumph. In the words of the originators, players, and supporters alike: "Vamos, Inter Miami!" The journey isn't over; it's a ceaseless voyage from vision to victory, and the pages of this chronicle are but a preface to the stories however to unfurl.

With appreciation for the shared travel.

www.ingramcontent.com/pod-product-compliance
Lightning Source LLC
Chambersburg PA
CBHW050044260726
48658CB00005B/1771